WORKSHOP ELVES ARE OFF THE SHELVES!

LINEWORK PATTERN WORKBOOK

by Annie Lang

Annie's Elves are as busy as can be getting everything ready for Santa's big night! Share the fun and choose from dozens of mix and match themed character designs created from Annie's Christmas Elves and Santa's Workshop collection of images. Many of the elf images were used to create Annie's "A Little Elf Upon a Shelf" Holiday Storybook which makes this pattern book a "MUST" for any creative holiday elf!

Simply trace the design and then transfer the image onto your project surface to make outstanding personalized items with professional results every time.

Transferring the linework designs

Trace the design of your choice with pencil and tracing paper. Place transfer paper under the tracing paper and place onto your selected surface. Hold in place with tape if necessary. Retrace over the linework to transfer the design onto the project. For fabrics, trace the design, flip the pattern over and retrace the lines using a fabric transfer pen. Follow manufacturer's direction to iron the design onto your chosen fabric item.

Color or paint these designs with

Craft paints, watercolors, markers, coloring pencils, chalks, inks, fabric pens, paint pens, or crayons

These designs are great for

Home Dec Items like furniture, cabinets, accent items, walls, lamps, glassware, kitchen accessories, office and desk items, bathroom accents, cabinets, patio pots and outdoor items, etc.
Fabric and wearable items like t-shirts, sweatshirts, aprons, canvas shoes, totes, quilting squares, table linens and napkins, window and shower curtains, pillows, etc.
Paper Craft Projects like greeting cards, scrap page elements, tags, labels, stationery items, ornaments, gift bags, etc.

For more ideas and designer tips, please visit my Blog at
http://annielang-anniethingspossible.blogspot.com/
My Pinterest Board at http://www.pinterest.com/anniethings/
or my Facebook Page at
http://www.facebook.com/anniethingspossible

Santa's
Workshop
Elves

(C) Annie Lang
anniethingspossible.com

Santa's Workshop Elves

(C) Annie Lang
anniethingspossible.com

Santa's
Workshop Elves

Santa's Workshop Elves

(C) Annie Lang anniethingspossible.com

Santa's Workshop Elves

Santa's Workshop Elves

(C) Annie Lang
anniethingspossible.com

Santa's Workshop Elves

Santa's Workshop Elves

Santa's Workshop Elves

*You can also use these toy maker elves
with the shelves and bench patterns
found in the Santa's Workshop Workbook!*

(C) Annie Lang
anniethingspossible.com

NAILS

NAILS

Santa's Workshop Elves

*You can also use these gift wrapping elves
with the shelves and bench patterns
found in the Santa's Workshop Workbook!*

Santa's Workshop Elves

*You can also use these doll making elves with the toy shelves and bench patterns found in the Santa's Workshop Workbook!

(C) Annie Lang
anniethingspossible.com

Santa's
Workshop Elves

(C) Annie Lang
anniethingspossible.com

*You can use the candy canes and worker
elves to create perpetual borders!

Santa's Workshop
(C) Annie Lang anniethingspossible.com

Image to use to create workshop scene Toy Shelf

Santa's Workshop

(C) Annie Lang anniethingspossible.com

Image to use to create workshop scene Gift Shop Shelf

Santa's Workshop

Image to use to create workshop Elf Shelf scene

Santa's Workshop

(C) Annie Lang anniethingspossible.com

These signs fit over workshop benches or over workshop shelf images

this sign fits over workshop building door

Santa's Workshop (C) Annie Lang anniethingspossible.com

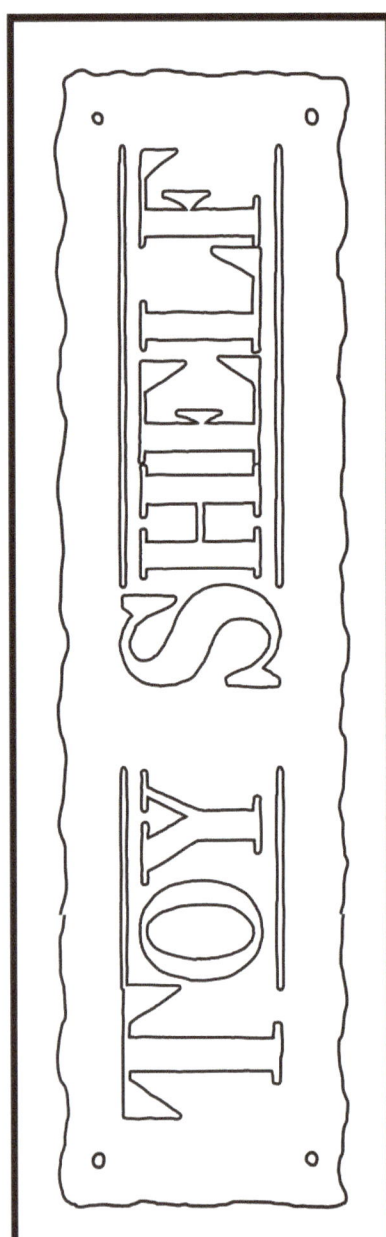

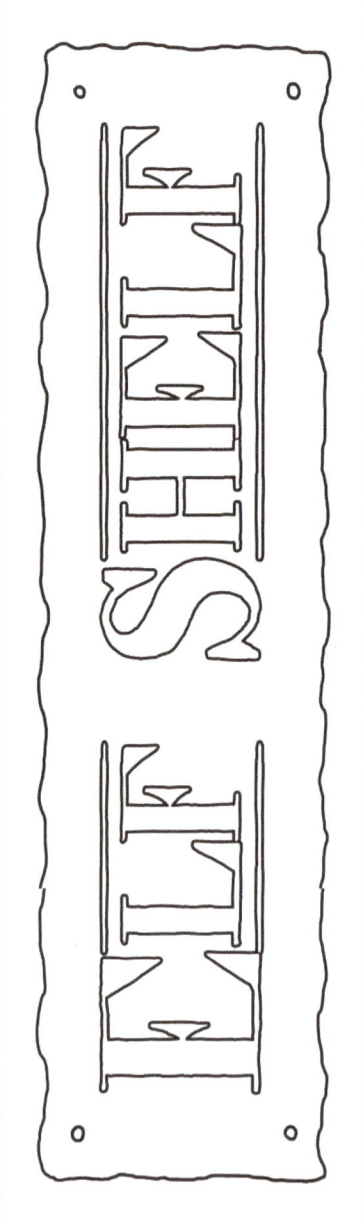

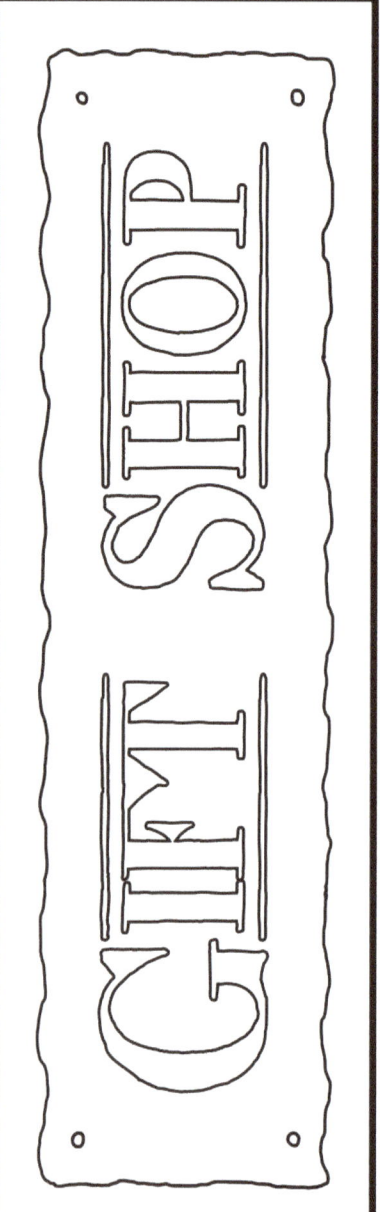

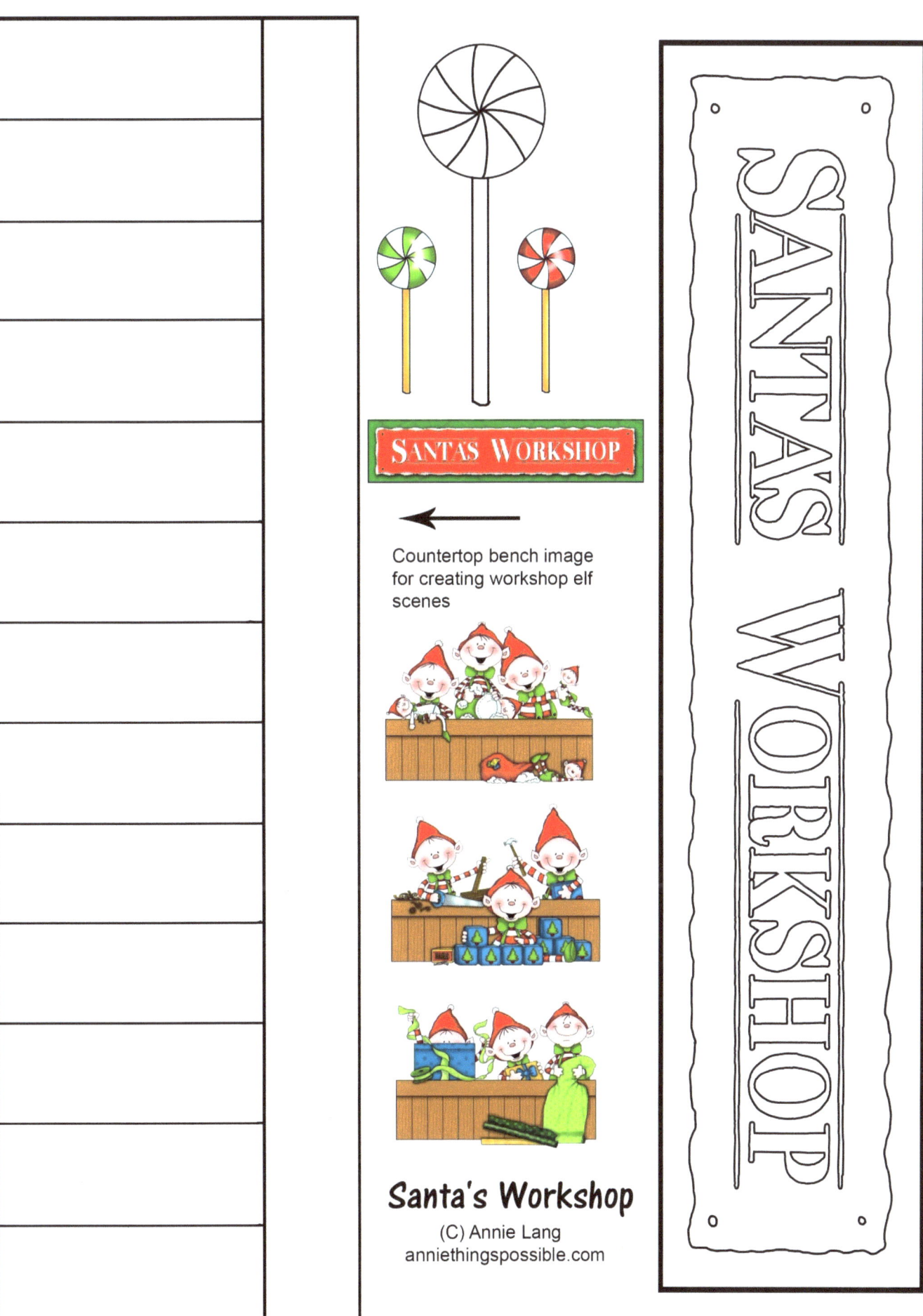

SANTA'S WORKSHOP

Countertop bench image for creating workshop elf scenes

Santa's Workshop

(C) Annie Lang
anniethingspossible.com

SANTA'S WORKSHOP

Background to use to create workshop scenes   **Santa's Workshop**   (C) Annie Lang anniethingspossible.com

Horizontal background to use to create workshop scenes   **Santa's Workshop**   (C) Annie Lang anniethingspossible.com

Santa's Workshop

Santa's Workshop

Santa's Workshop

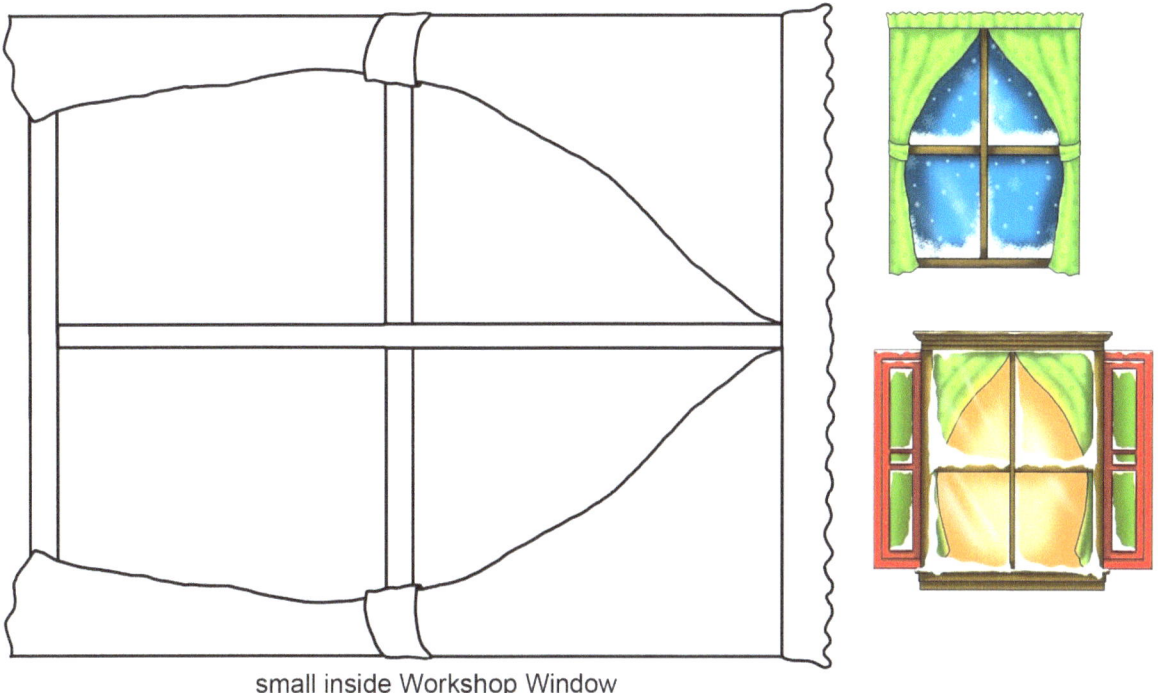

small inside Workshop Window

Santa's Workshop
(C) Annie Lang anniethingspossible.com

small outside Workshop Window

Large Workshop Window Scene

Santa's Workshop

Santa's Workshop

(C) Annie Lang
anniethingspossible.com

ANNIE LANG'S
HAPPY HOLIDAY ELVES

SPECIAL DELIVERY

ANNIE LANG'S

HAPPY HOLIDAY ELVES

Copyright (C) Annie Lang
anniethingspossible.com

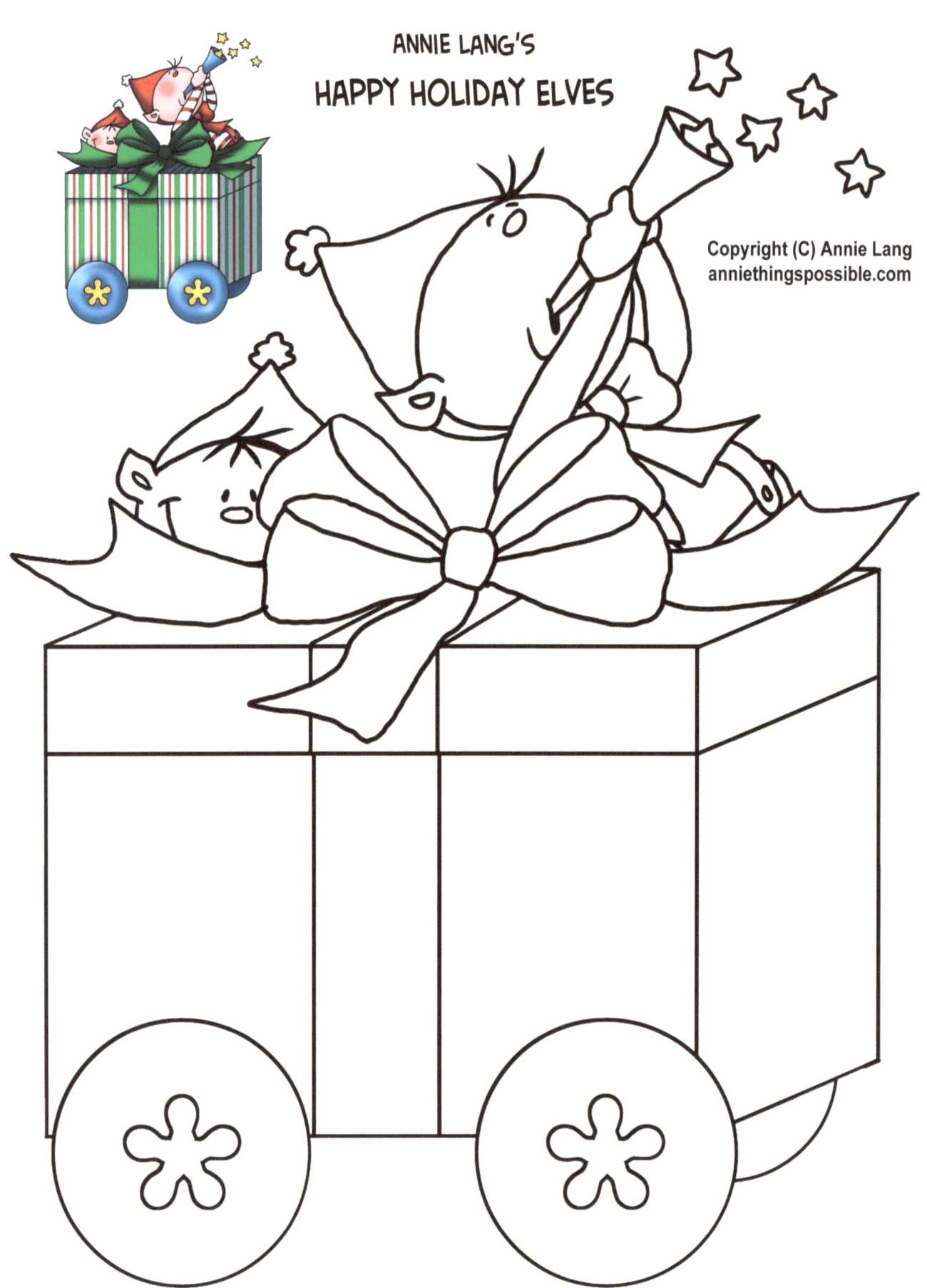

ANNIE LANG'S
HAPPY HOLIDAY ELVES

ANNIE LANG'S
HAPPY HOLIDAY ELVES

Copyright (C) Annie Lang
anniethingspossible.com

ANNIE LANG'S
HAPPY HOLIDAY ELVES

Copyright (C) Annie Lang
anniethingspossible.com

ANNIE LANG'S
HAPPY HOLIDAY ELVES

ANNIE LANG'S
HAPPY HOLIDAY ELVES

ANNIE LANG'S
HAPPY HOLIDAY ELVES

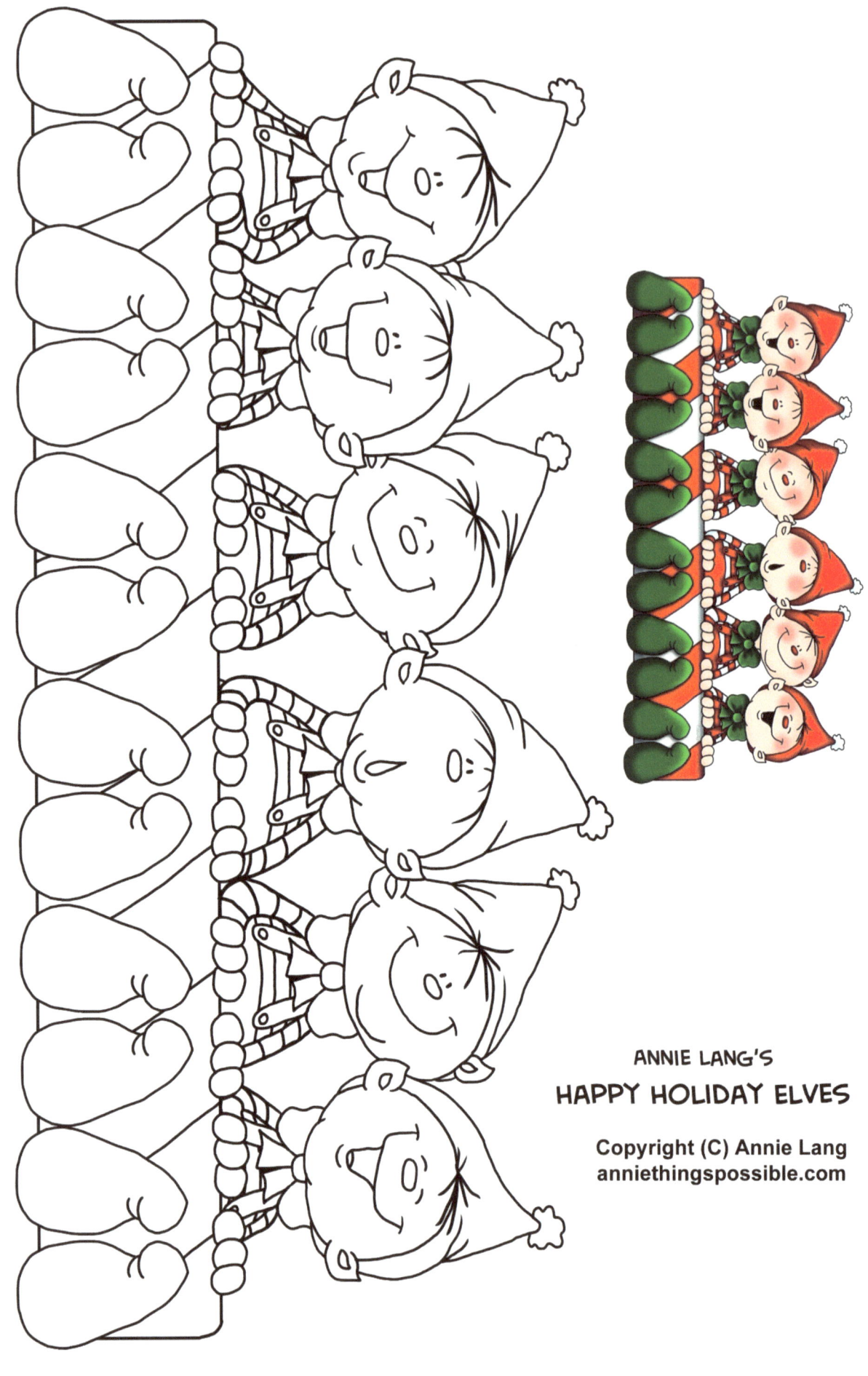

ANNIE LANG'S
HAPPY HOLIDAY ELVES

Copyright (C) Annie Lang
anniethingspossible.com

ANNIE LANG'S
HAPPY HOLIDAY ELVES

notes and memos

(C) Annie Lang annielangsbooks.com

Thank you for purchasing this publication!

Find dozens of other fun titles on my
Annie Lang's Books website!

I hope you enjoyed this book and
encourage you to leave a review and share your
thoughts for other customers at Amazon.com!

To learn more about the author, get free project
ideas, see video how-to's and more, please visit
Annie Lang's BLOG at
http://annielang-anniethingspossible.blogspot.com/

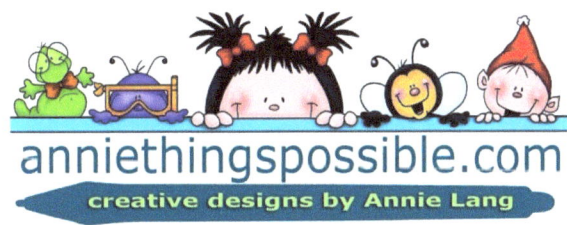

www.ingramcontent.com/pod-product-compliance
Lightning Source LLC
Chambersburg PA
CBHW041524280526

45792CB00004B/1375